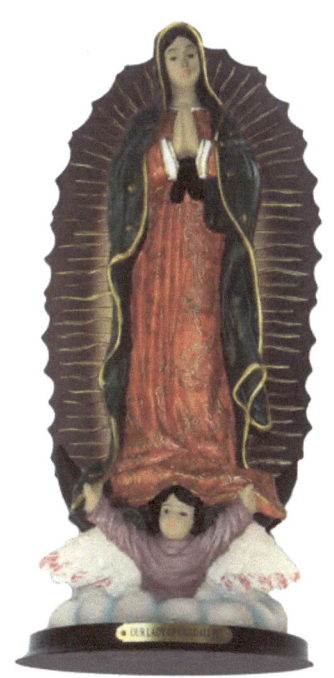

1

## WYLIE'S WERKSTÄTTE: THE NEW COMFORT ZONE

*Would you like to wait here in the sitting room or sit here in the waiting room? – Firesign Theatre*

We spend a considerable chunk of our existence(s) sitting and waiting, waiting for doctors, lawyers, clients, (potential) employers, jury foremen, auto repairmen, planes, trains, restaurant seats, ad infinitum. Why do we dread such down time? Because everything about the spaces in which we wait reinforces our sense of suspension, our sense of lost time, our sense that, no matter what work or reading we manage to accomplish in these interstices, we are doing nothing but aging. We sit in waiting rooms.

Cynthia Wylie would have us wait in sitting rooms. She re-Imagines the transitional space as a welcoming locus, a warm and lively-looking environment whose smart and charming details are boldly described and, ultimately, reassuring, reintroducing natural forces otherwise conspicuous by their absence. It doesn't matter whether these handsome prints and delicate images define a public or a private room; they enliven the domestic setting no less than the common.

And, of course, these apparitions do not confine themselves to the walls. They climb down and insinuate themselves about and beside us, inflecting the objects that might surround us. Together they propose a gracious atmosphere, a lucid and unified "through-composition" that satisfies the intellect with its coherence even as it gratifies the senses with its sober beauty.

Wylie's approach to design – her dedication to an integrated approach to interior elaboration no less than her complex but highly ordered and carefully stylized "language of form" – harks back to concepts and styles we regard as from a much different time and place. But, if we know that the decorous yet sensuous approaches of Art Nouveau, the Craftsman style, and the Wiener Werkststätte – not to mention their progeny, including Art Deco and the Bauhaus – are the day-before-yesterday's avant garde, we find that the spirit, and even the manner(s), they unleashed upon a thirsty world a century ago not only remain fresh, but quench the same thirst now. Everything old is new again – and not a moment too soon.

One thing Wylie does that inherits so directly from high-Modernist hip is work and think as an artist and as a designer at the same time. She balances expressive impulse with imagined task, so that decorative detail re-imagines but grows directly out of delicately rendered image. The logic suffuses all the visual stimulation she provides us in her sitting-room concept(s). Each of her trees is at once a presence in and of itself and a source of attractively stylized symbolism. Each tree is not simply a unique figure, but a unique fount of genial heraldry. The pictures and the designs don't simply talk to one another, they grow out of and elucidate one another. Meaning, balance, symmetric relation pervades these room-proposals.

Who wouldn't want to sit here? Who would mind waiting here? Who would even want to leave? We wouldn't fall asleep in such vivacious surroundings, but we wouldn't be so damned eager to flee them, either. We would move onto our appointments with a certain regret, to be sure, but with refreshed purpose and sense of centeredness. And if we were entertaining or being entertained at home, we would indeed be entertained.

Call it win-win Werkstätte. Cynthia Wylie has rescued and renewed the transitional space, allowing us precisely the happy transit we need.

Peter Frank
Los Angeles                                                September 2010

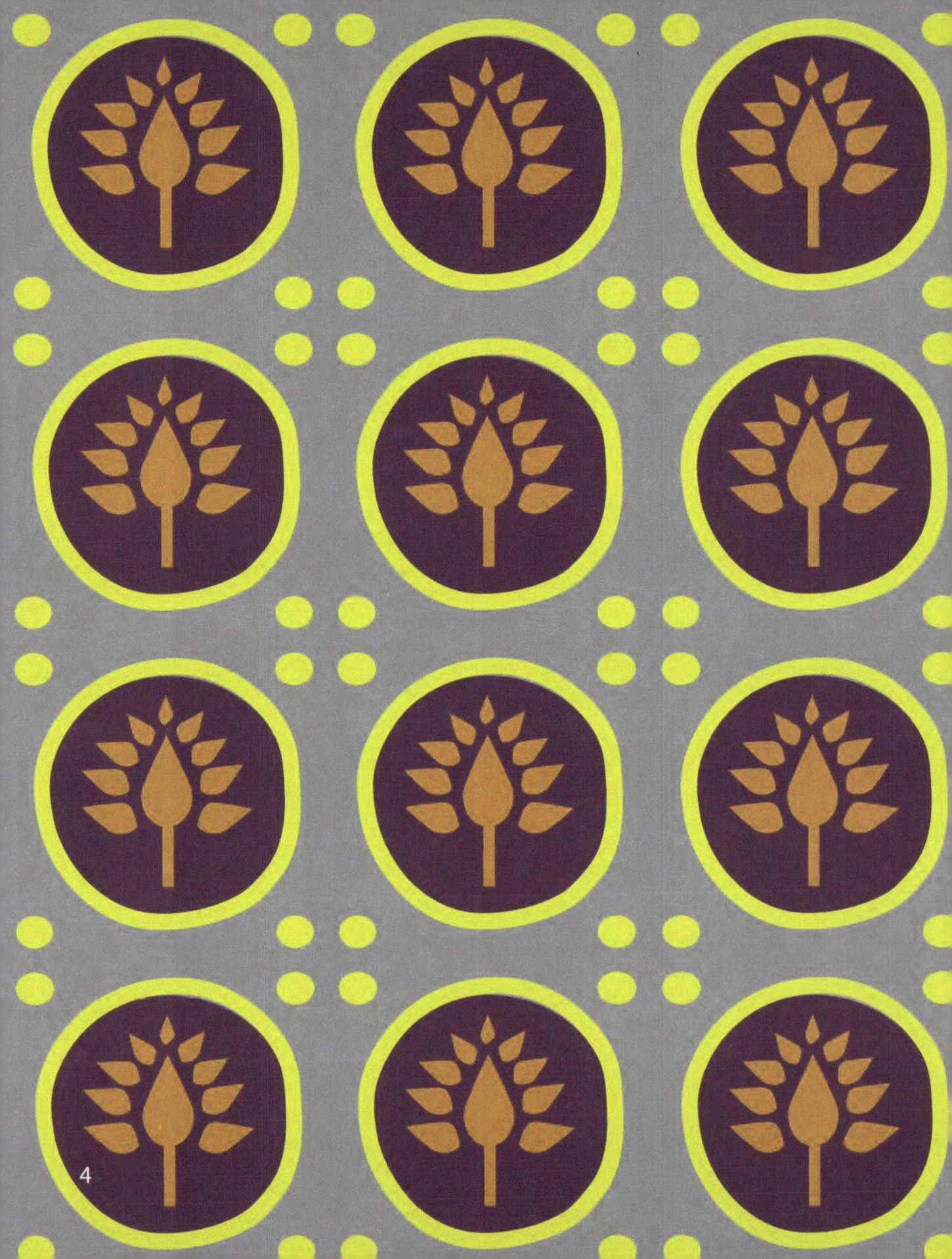

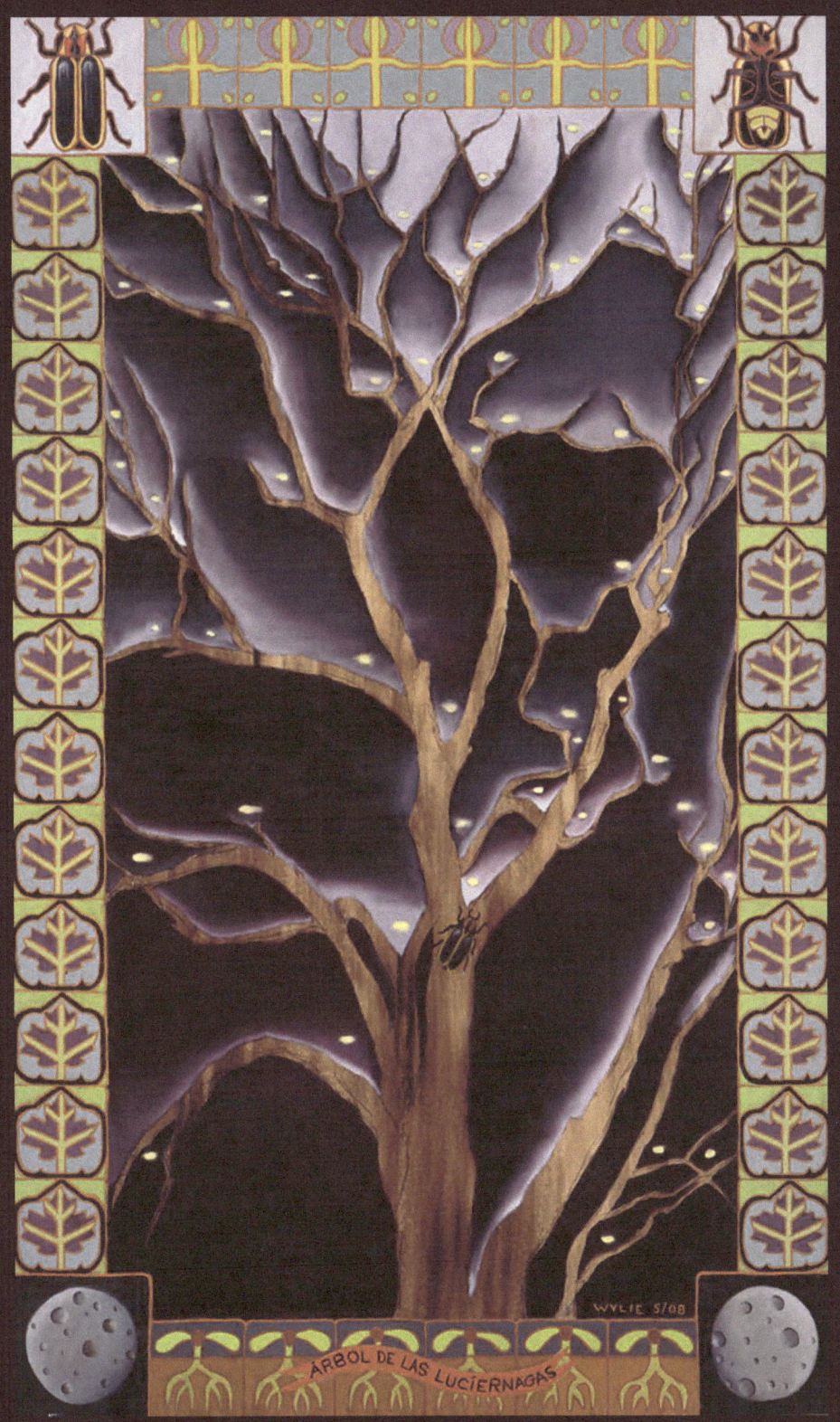

ARBOL DE LAS LUCIERNAGAS

Arbol de las Luciernagas II  ✿  Oil & Graphite on Canvas  ✿  36" x 60"

5

P + D means pattern and decoration and was dubbed by Holland Cotter of the New York times as: "…the last genuine art movement of the 20th century, which was also the first and only art movement of the postmodern era and may well prove to be the last art movement ever."

✍ January 15, 2008

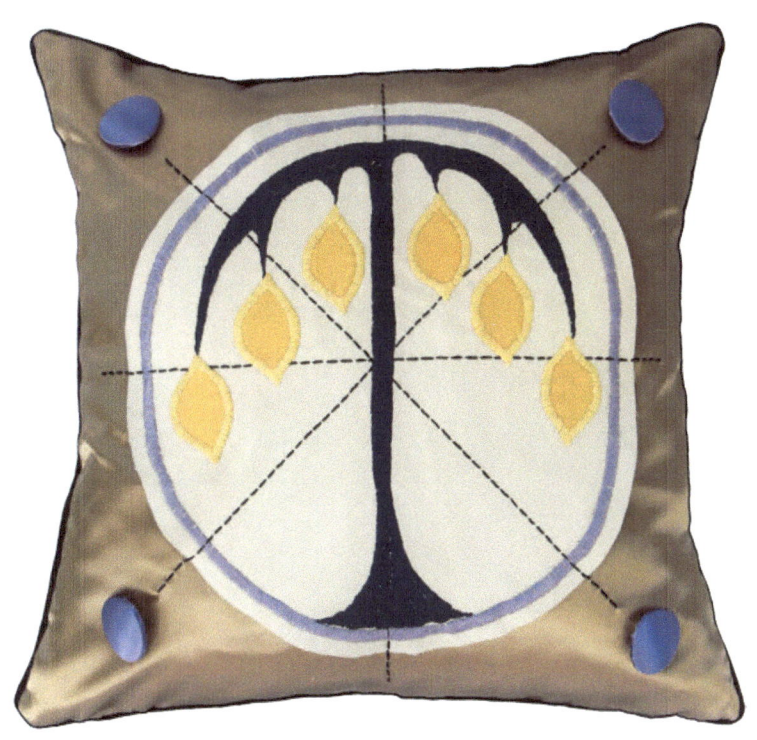

Lemon Tree Pillow   🌿   Satin, Suede, Embroidery   🌿   18" x 18"

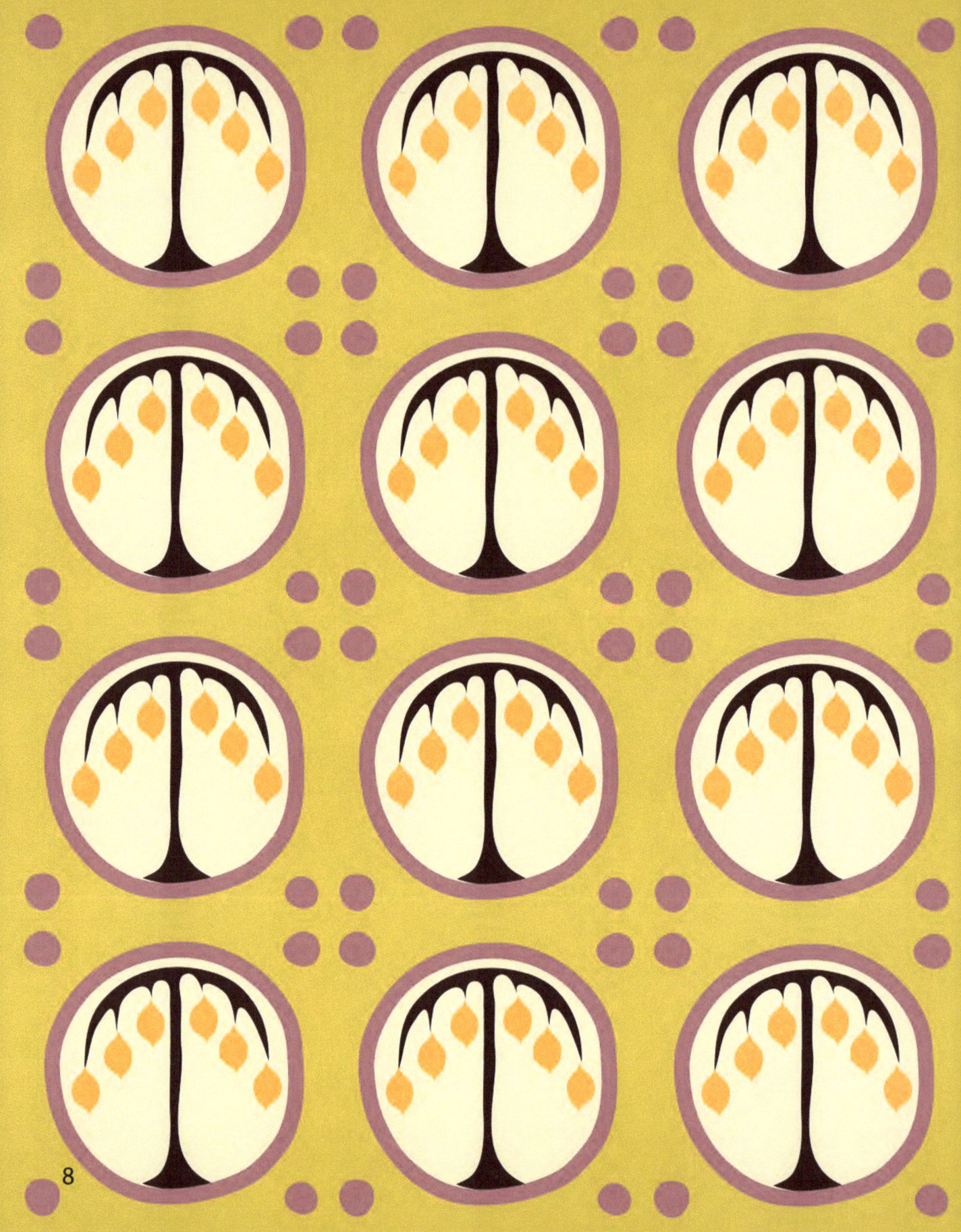

8

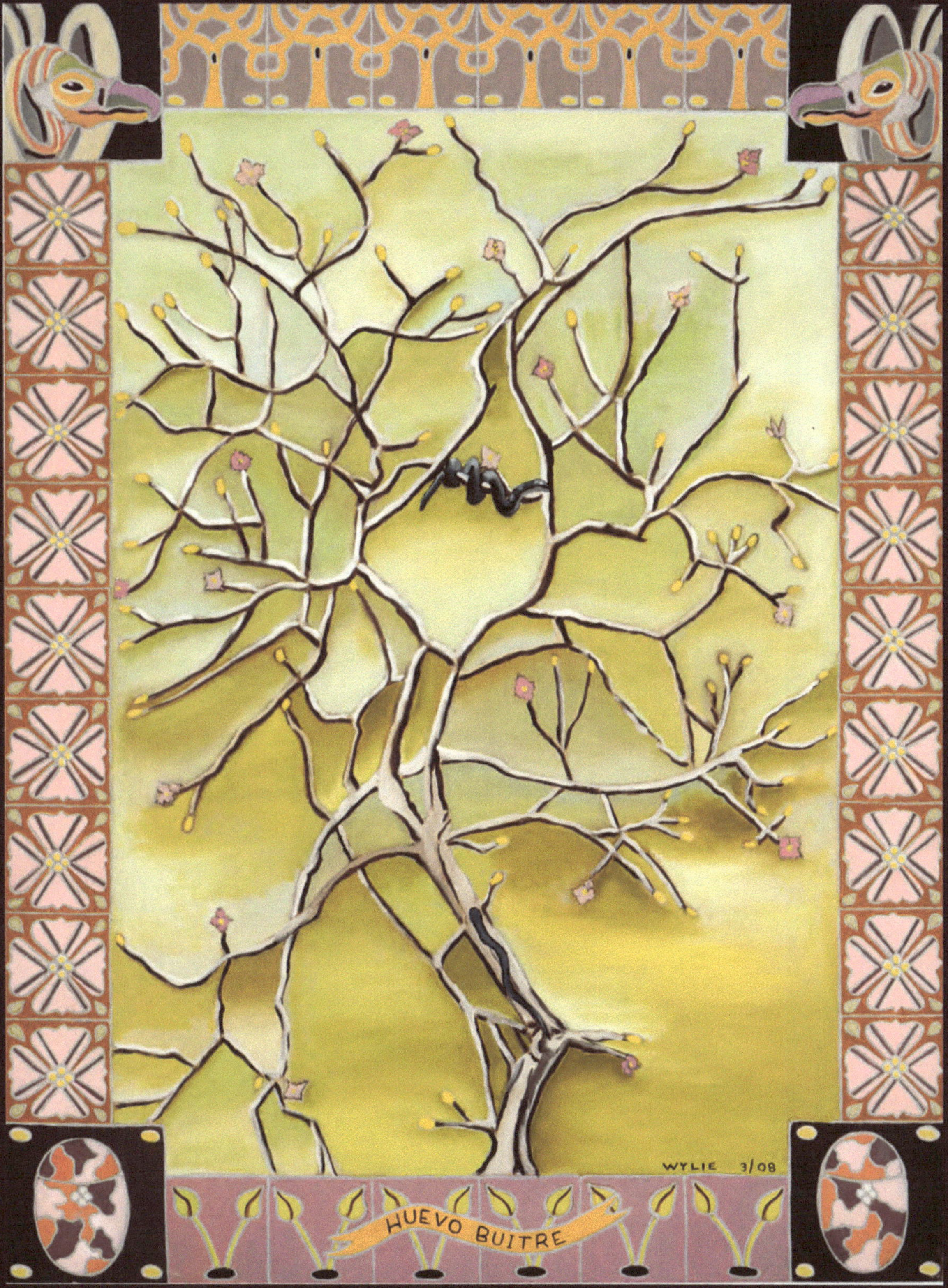

HUEVO BUITRE

WYLIE 3/08

Huevo Buitre  Oil on Canvas  36" x 48"

9

"I will talk to you of art,
for there is nothing else to talk about.
For there is nothing else.
Life is an obscure hobo
bumming a ride on the omnibus of art."

Maxwell H. Brock

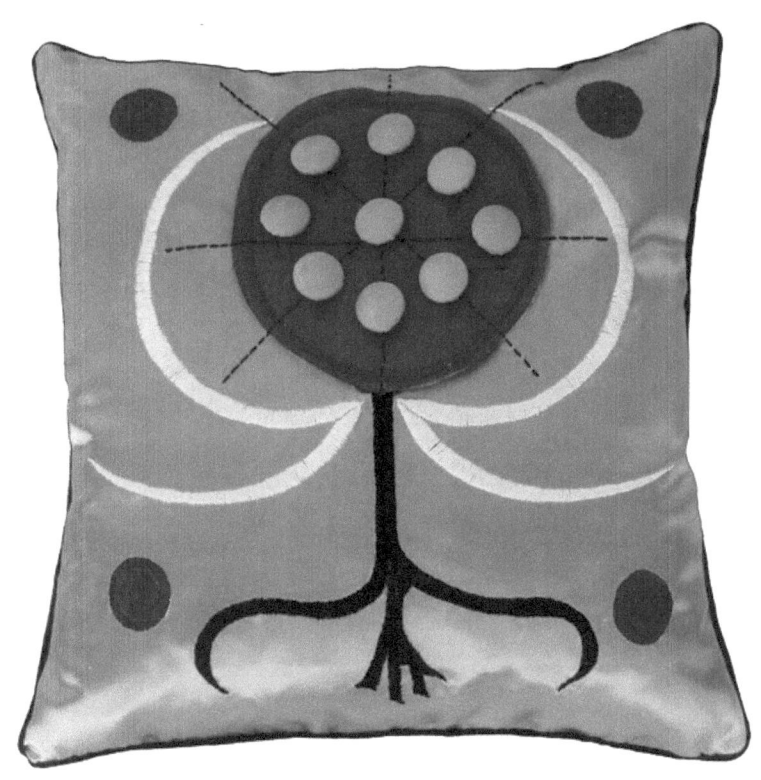

CloverTree Pillow  🍃  Satin, Suede, Embroidery  🍃  18" x 18"

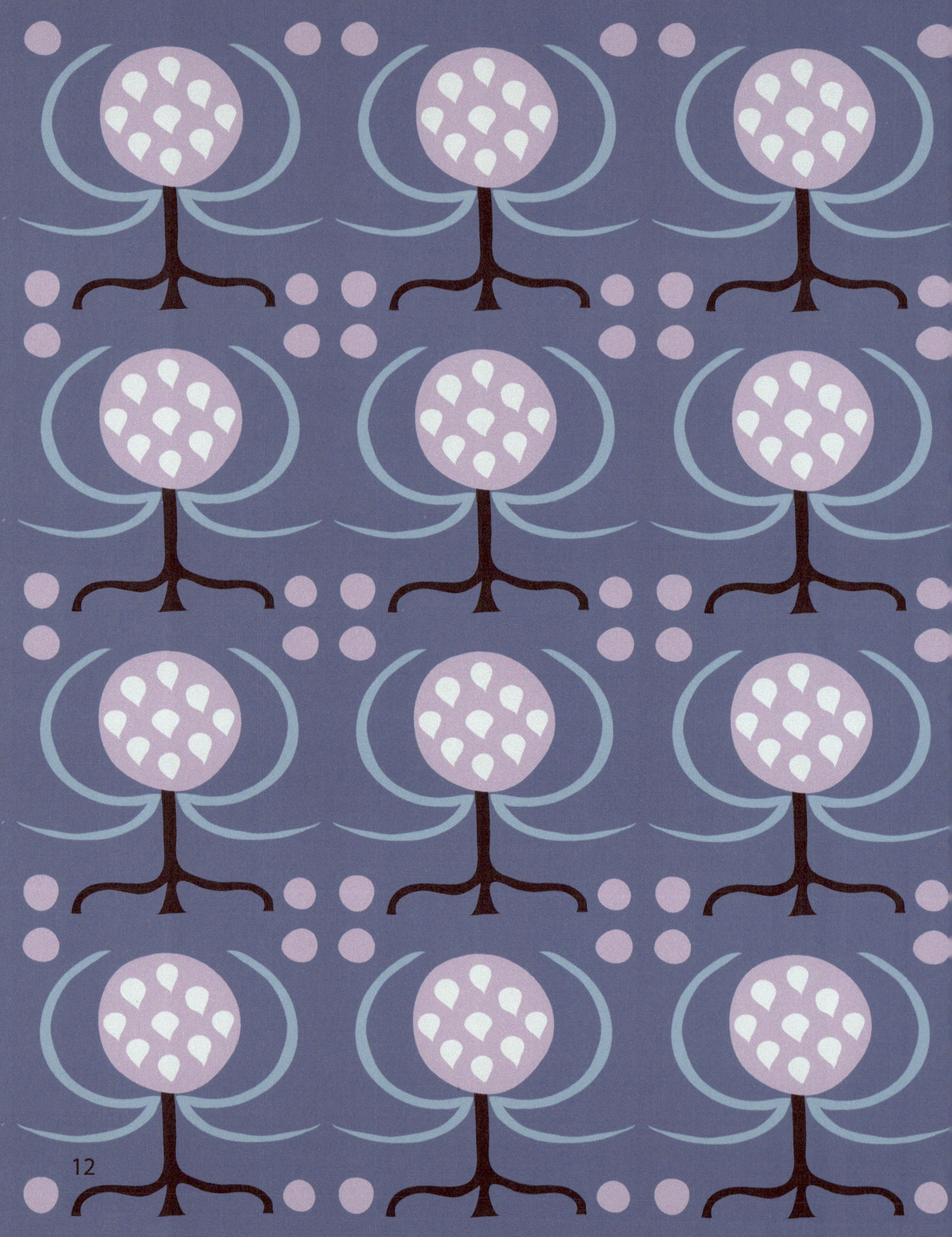

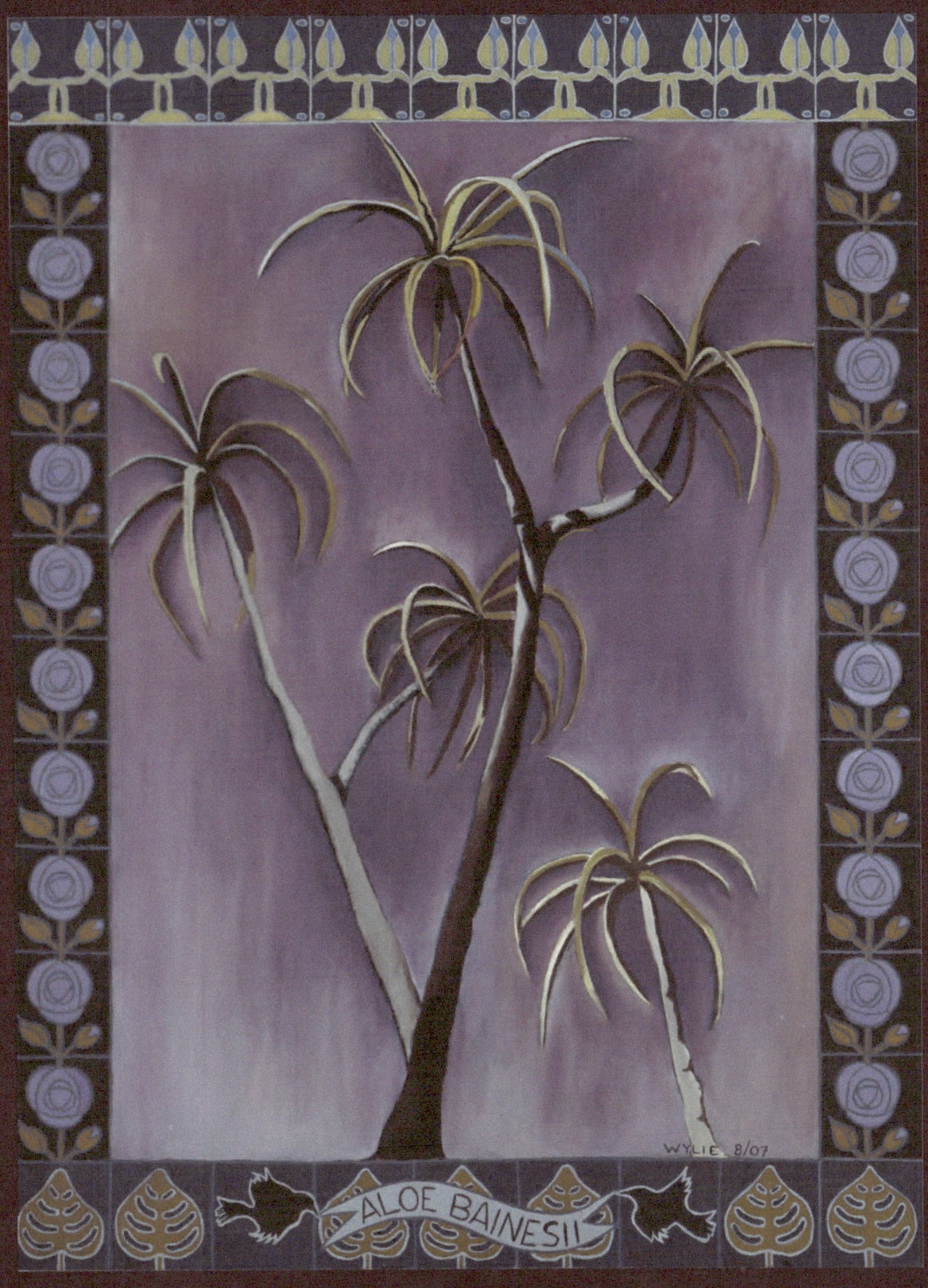

ALOE BAINESII

Aloe Bainesii ll 🍃 Oil on Canvas 🍃 36" x 48"

"Everything you can imagine is real."

⟋ Pablo Picasso

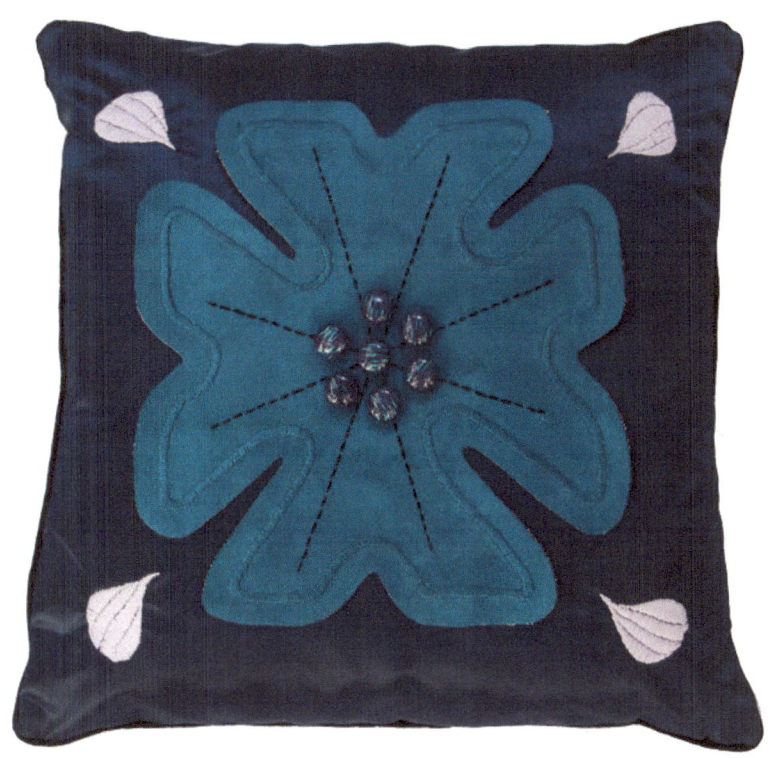

Bloomsberry Pillow   🌿   Satin, Suede, Embroidery   🌿   18" x 18"

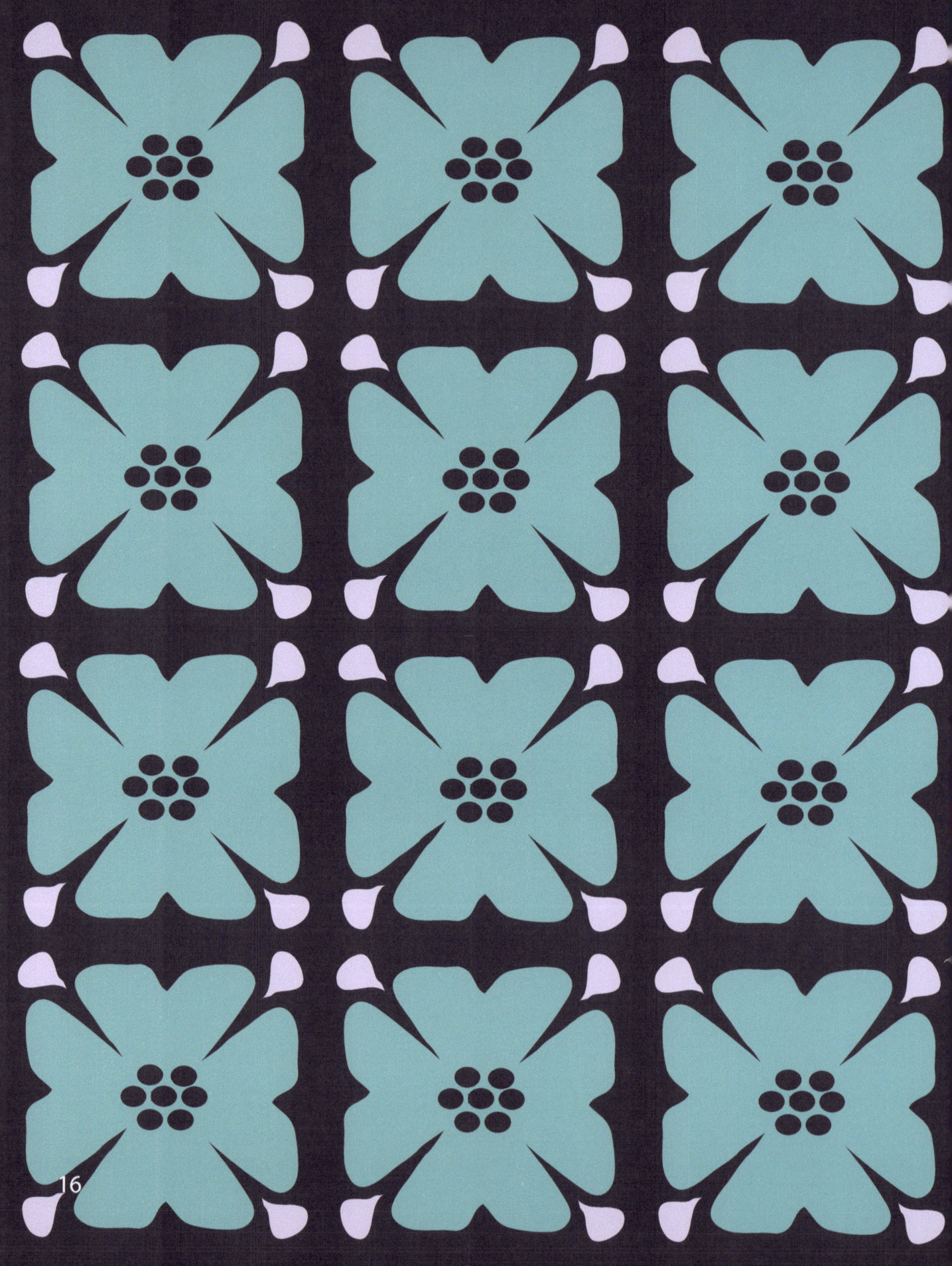

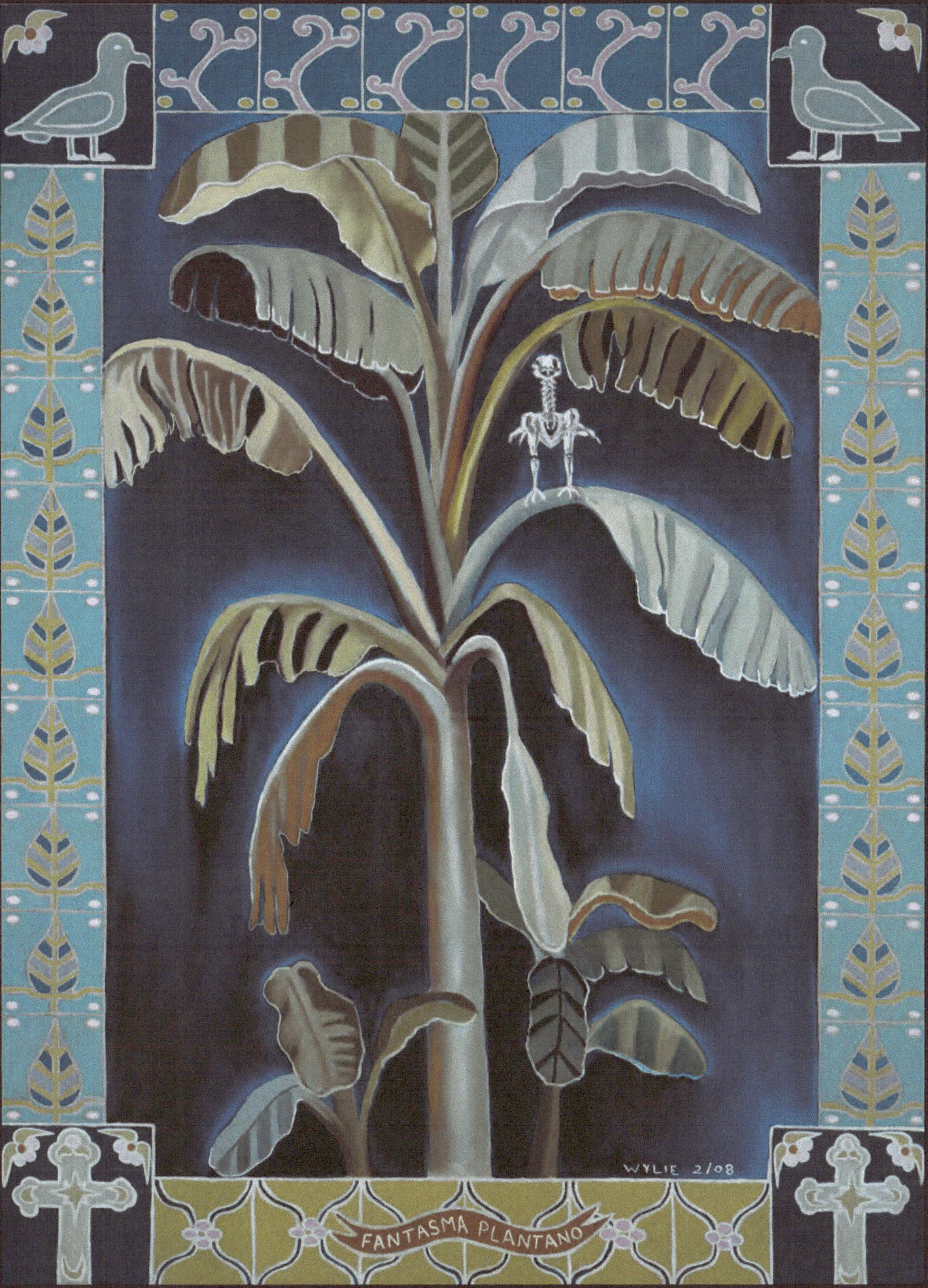


Fantasma Plantano II ❦ Oil on Canvas ❦ 36" x 48"

"What would you attempt to do
if you knew you could not fail?"

🖋 Unknown

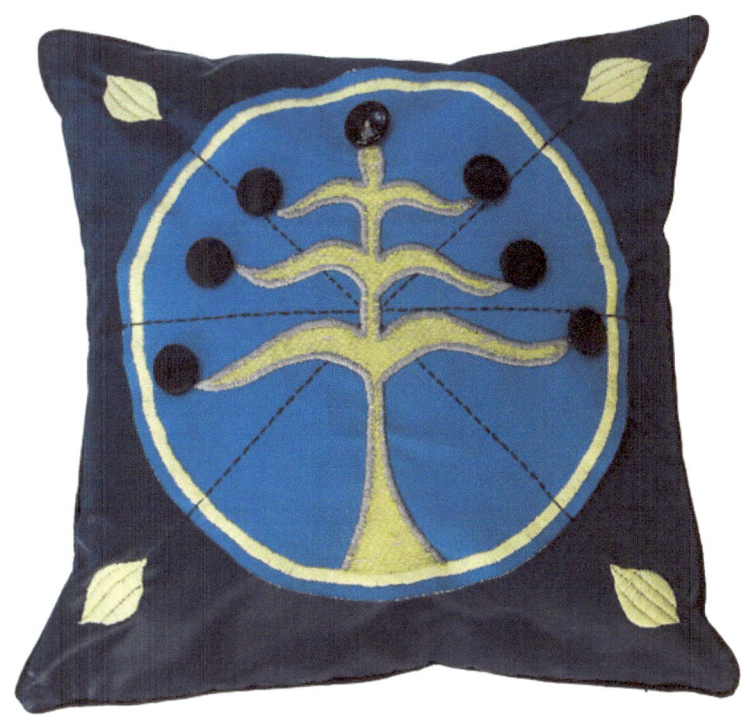

Olive Tree Pillow  🍃  Satin, Suede, Embroidery  🍃  18" x 18"

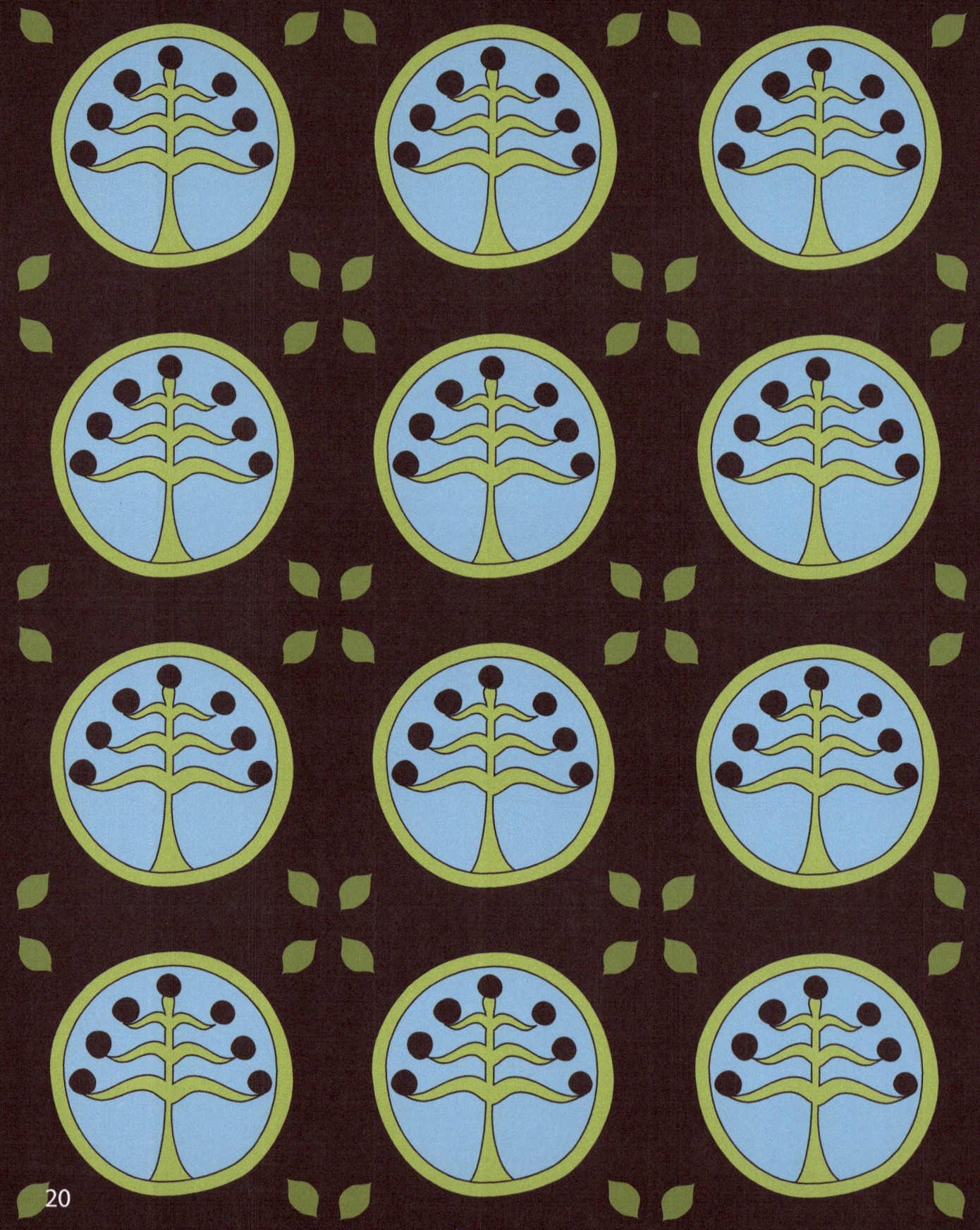

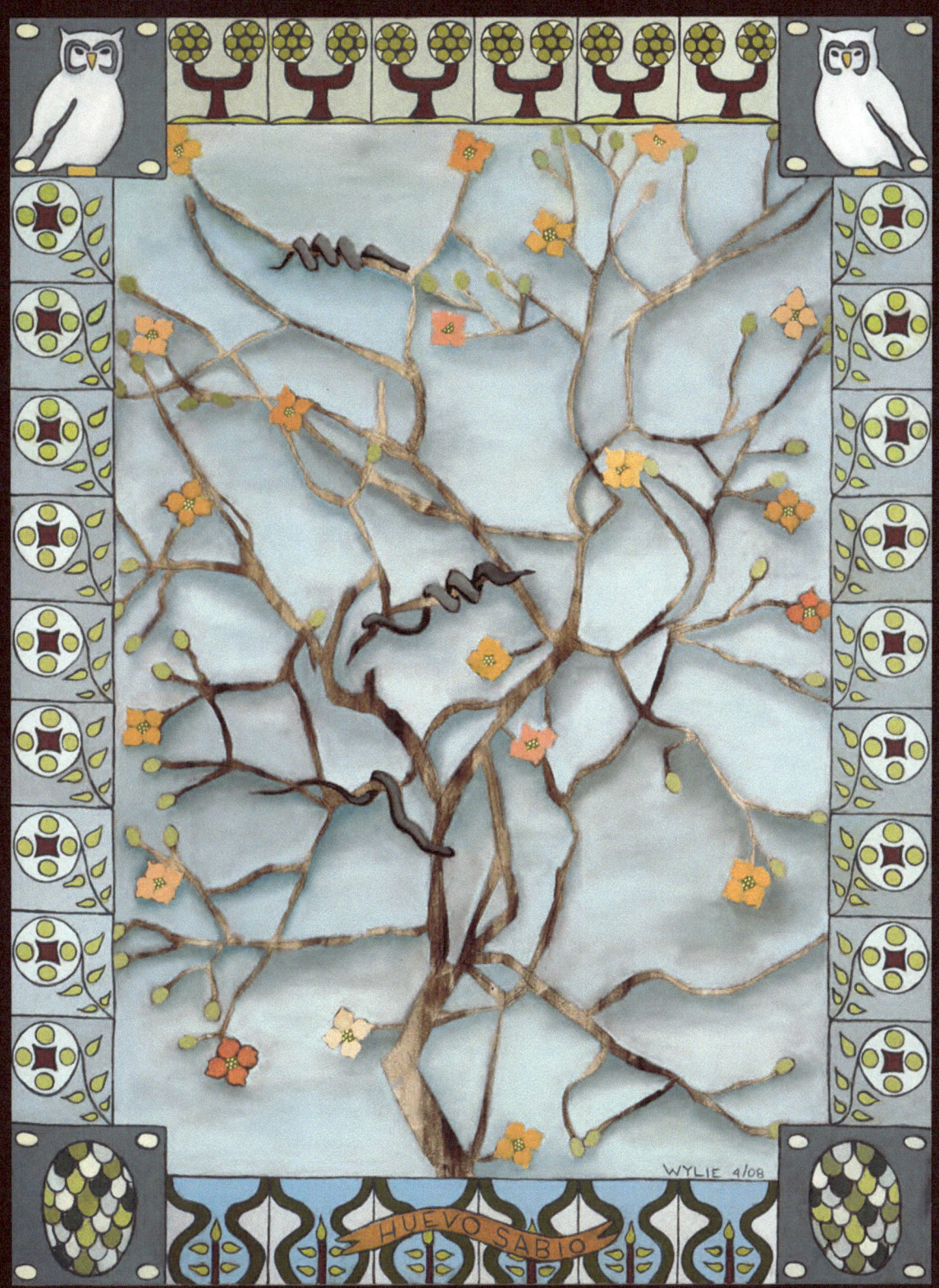

Huevo Sabio   🍃   Oil & Graphite on Canvas   🍃   36" x 48"

"An intellectual says a simple thing in a hard way.
An artist says a hard thing in a simple way."

⊘ Charles Bukowski

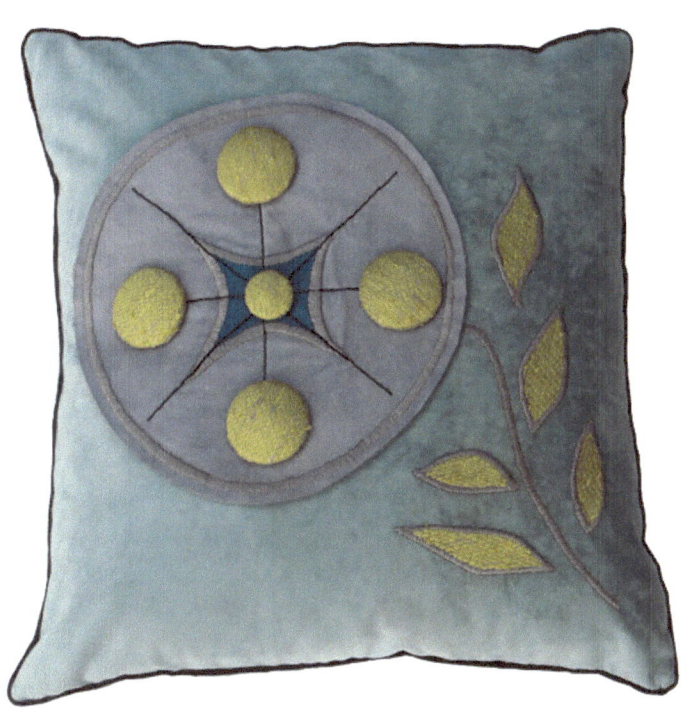

Seed Pod Pillow  🍃  Silk, Suede, Embroidery  🍃  18" x 18"

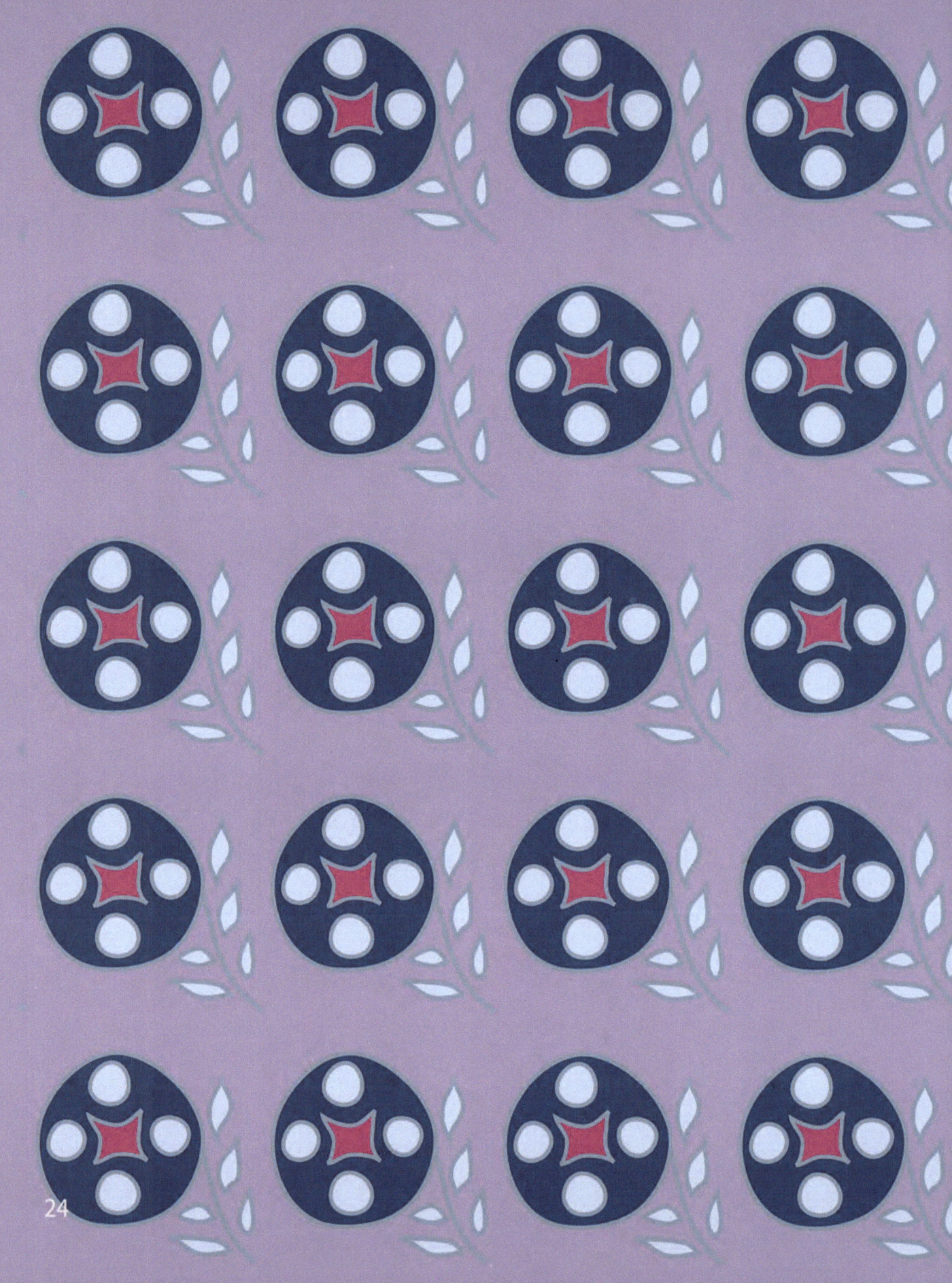

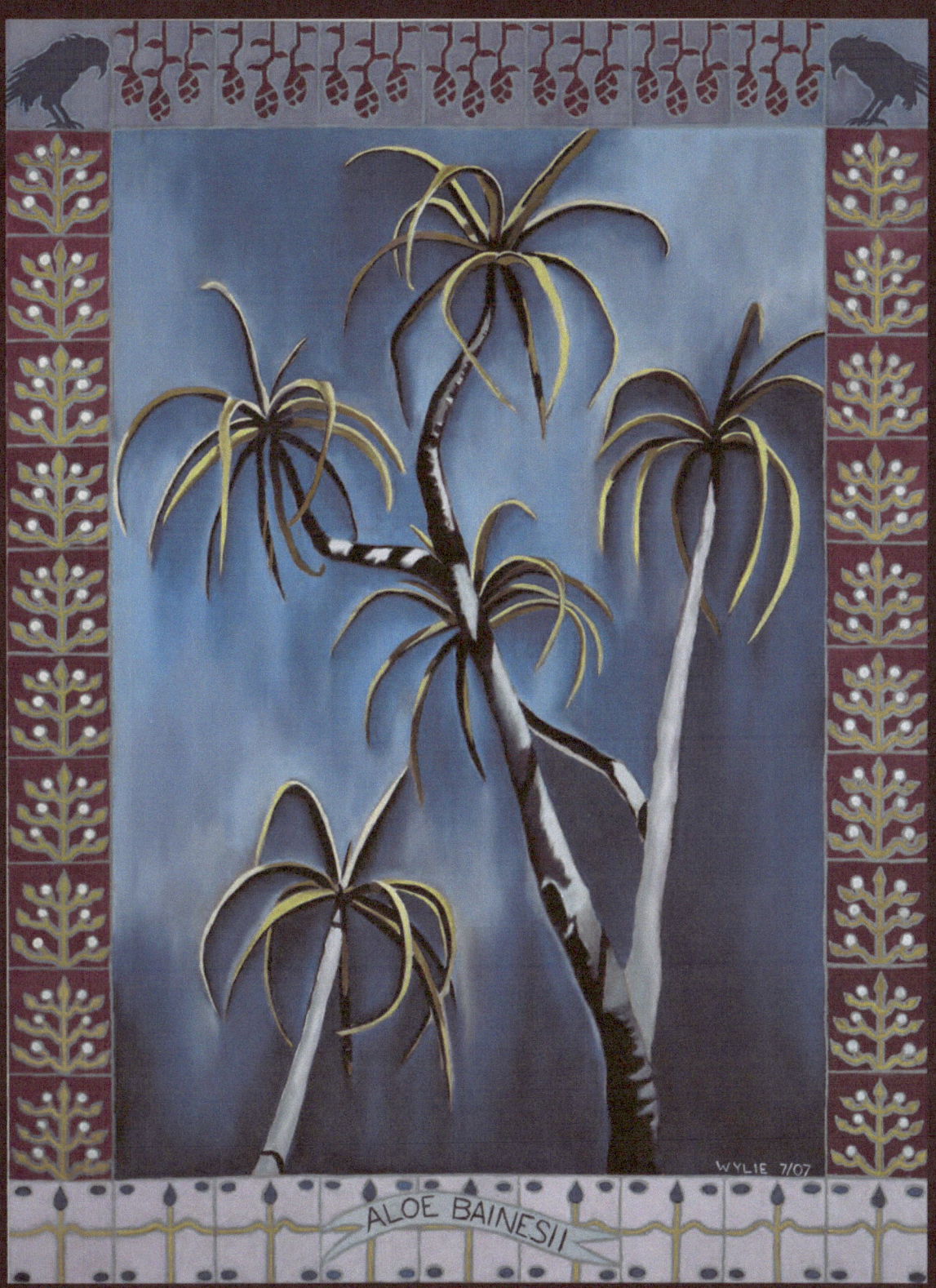

ALOE BAINESII

Aloe Bainesii 1   Oil & Graphite on Canvas   36" x 48"

In all endeavors I will aim to be:

Honorable ✍ Optimistic ✍ Resolute.

Cynthia Wylie
*Values Statement*

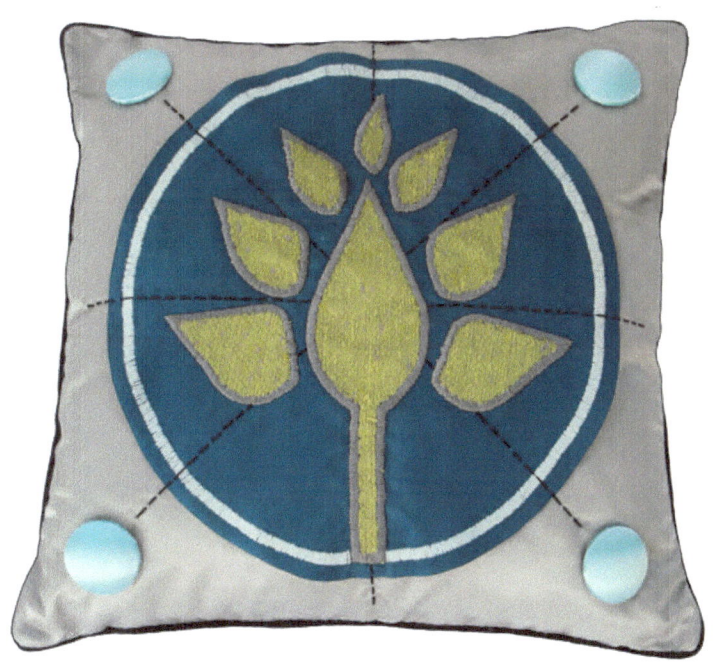

Pine Cone Pillow  🍃  Silk, Suede, Satin, Embroidery  🍃  18" x 18"

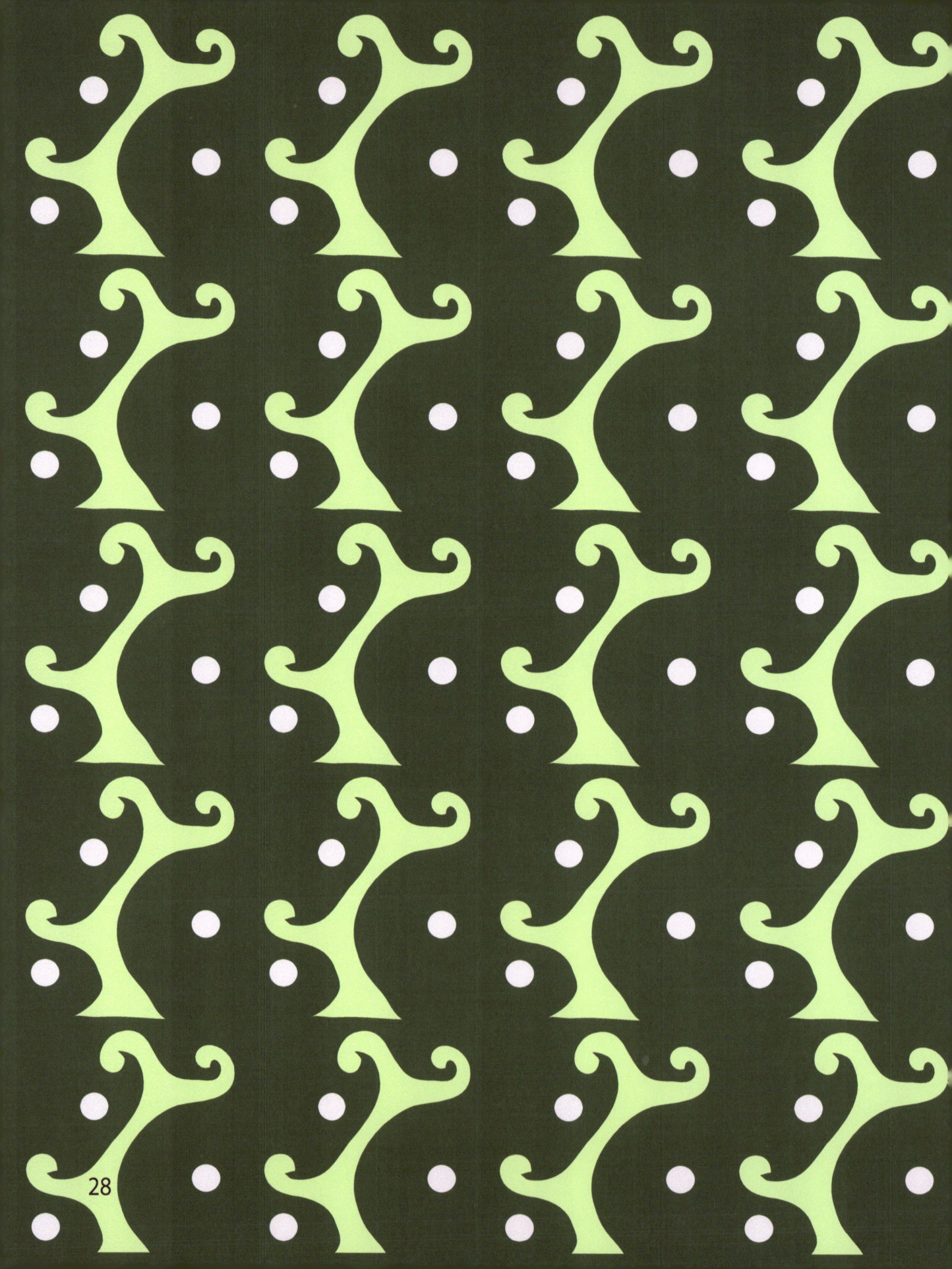

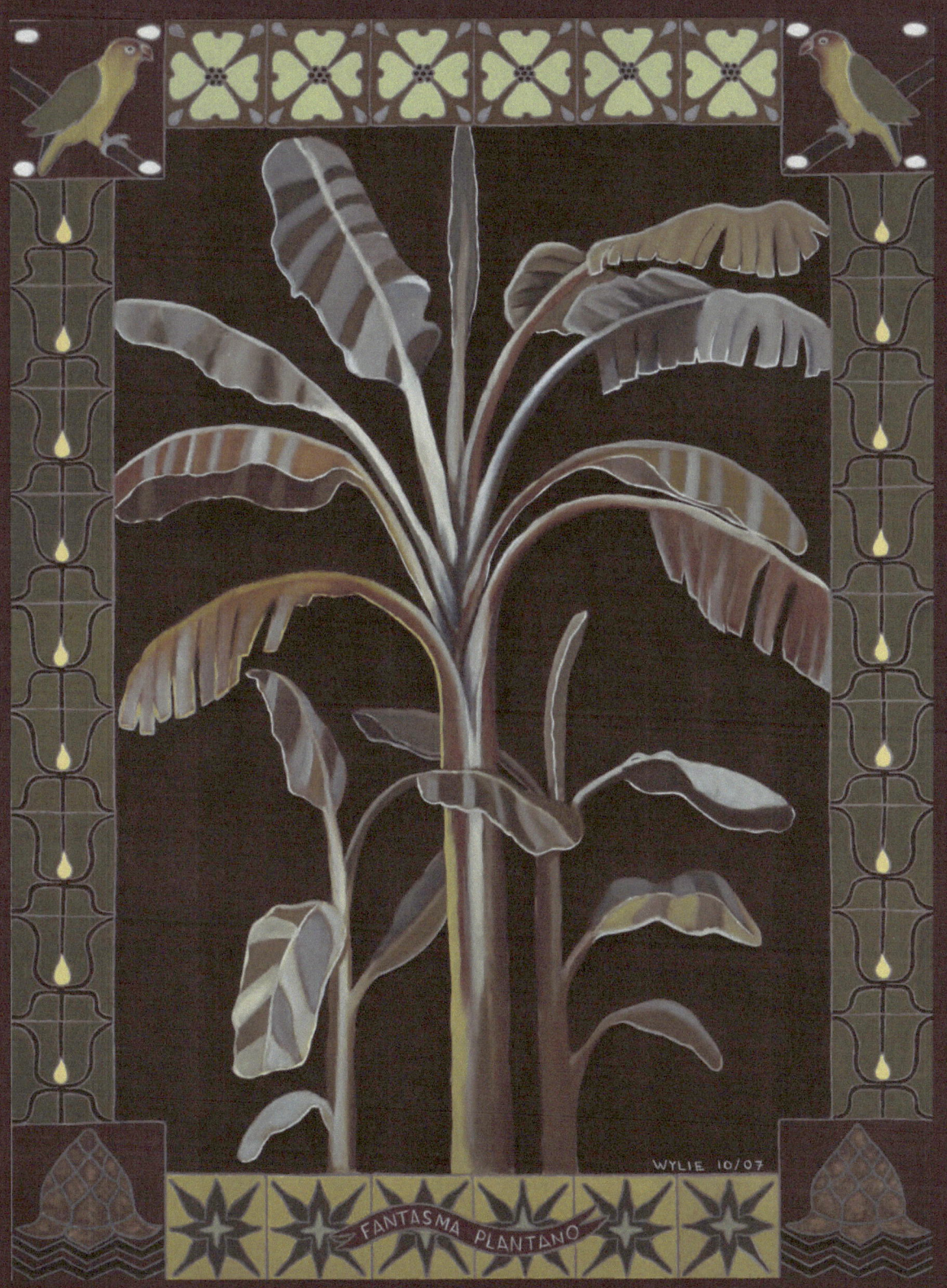

FANTASMA PLANTANO

WYLIE 10/07

Fantasma Plantano 1  🍃  Oil on Canvas  🍃  36" x 48"

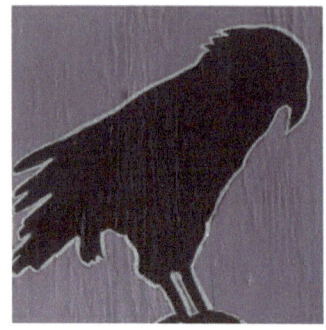
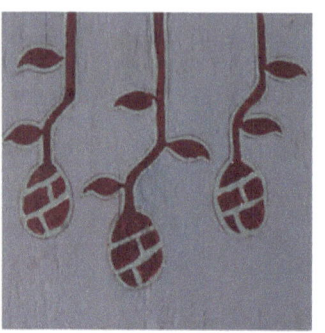
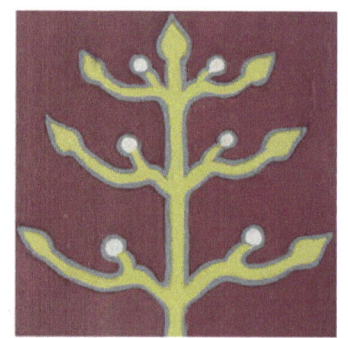
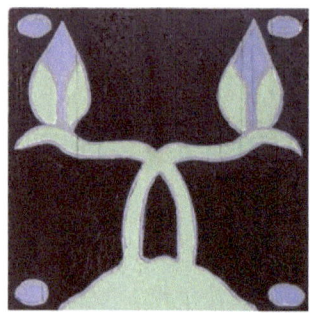
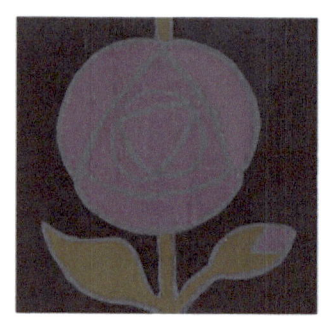
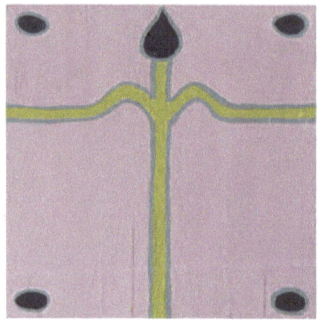
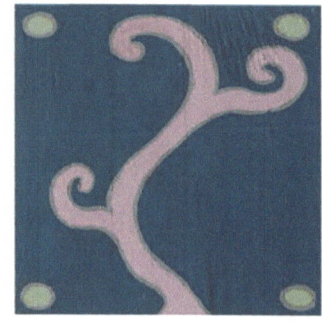
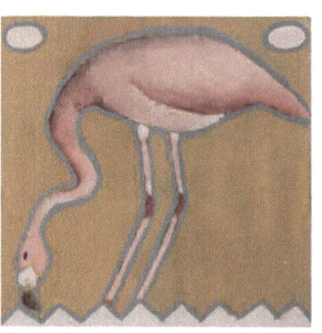

Pink Icons ✑ Oil on Plywood ✑ 6" x 6"

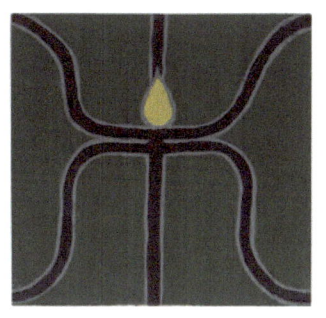
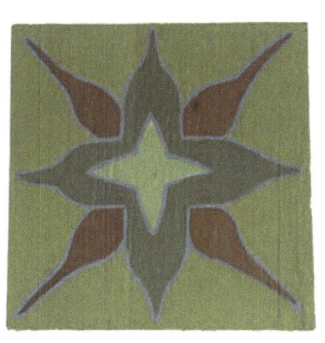

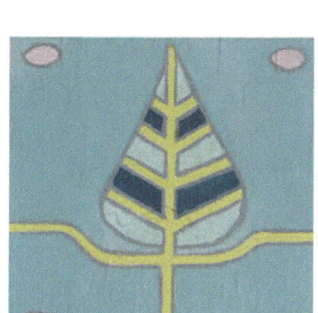
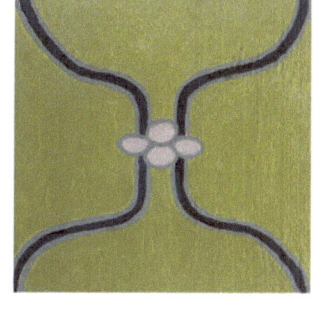
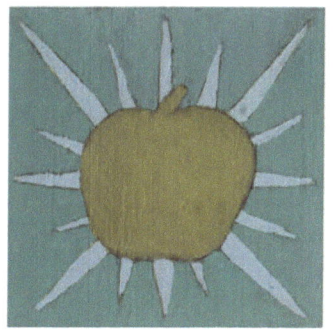
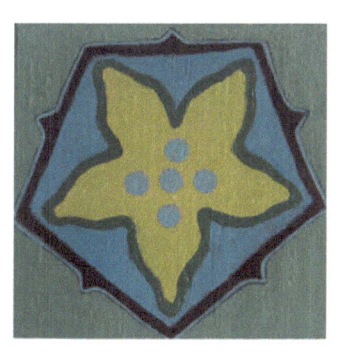

Green Icons   &#x2040;   Oil on Plywood   &#x2040;   6" x 6"

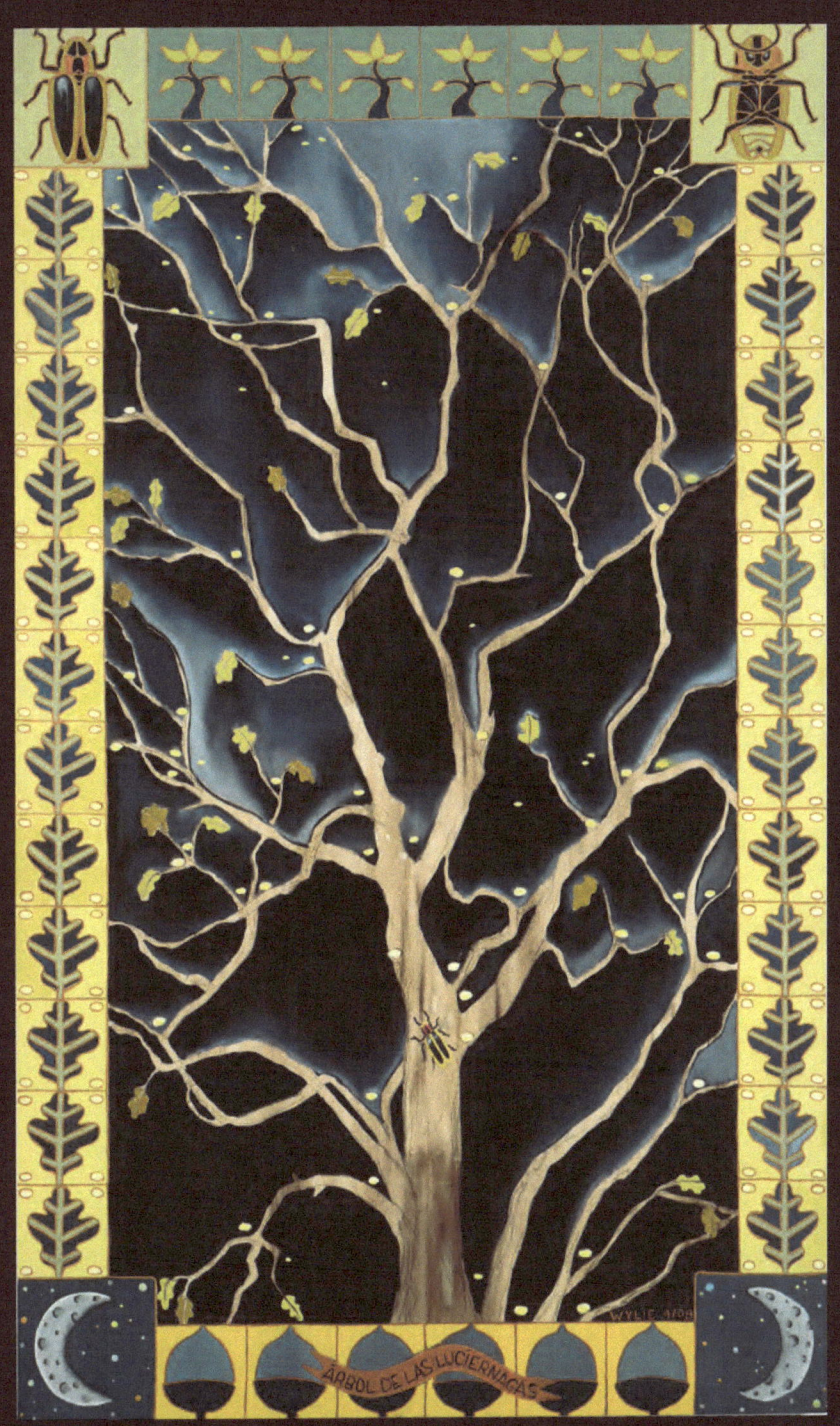

Árbol de las Luciernagas I  🌿  Oil & Graphite on Canvas  🌿  36" x 60"

To Be or Not to Be

In an effort to distance myself from my heritage, I moved 3000 miles away.  It didn't work.  I never considered that what lurked between my genetics would matter.  But there it was, inhabiting my creative self, becoming stronger every day.

What I learned as a kid in my mom's neighborhood 'Embroidery Bees';  what I saw growing up as my mom silently embroidered; what I was taught as a youngster and my firm position then - that I didn't want any part of it – didn't have any bearing on my outcome, after all.

Funny how that works.  A strange kind of voodoo exists that I am well aware is of great importance to what makes me an artist.


               Mick Bender

Why I Paint

It renders me worthy. I contribute something good to the world. It makes my legacy richer. I can give my paintings to friends and family.

It is fun to squeeze paint from a tube. I love mixing colors. I love juxtaposing unusual colors in surprising ways to see how they will look together. I can make something more beautiful than it is.

Simplifying the world around me is soothing. I can add order to my life.

Painting is exhausting and gratifying like exercise. I can be physical.

Trees are alive too. Trees have a life. They may be the key to our survival. I can send a message into the world.

I see the birds. I hear the fountain. I can listen to music and drink fine wine when I paint. I can stand outside all day.

It satisfies my drive for accomplishment. I can finish a painting.

My paintings look beautiful on my walls. Like a ghost from the past, I can remember a scene I once thought meaningful.

✍ Cynthia Wylie

Acknowledgments:

Evan MacKenzie
Mick Bender
Dean Harada
Delia Cabral
Peter Frank
Brent Turner
Willard Ford
Samuel Moyer
Eli Bonerz
1HappyCleaners
Friends + Family